New and Selected Poems

First published in 2011 by
Liberties Press
Guinness Enterprise Centre | Taylor's Lane | Dublin 8
Tel: +353 (1) 415 1224
www.libertiespress.com | info@libertiespress.com

Trade enquiries to Gill & Macmillan Distribution
Hume Avenue | Park West | Dublin 12
Tel: +353 (1) 500 9534 | Fax: +353 (1) 500 9595
sales@gillmacmillan.ie

Distributed in the United States by
Dufour Editions | PO Box 7 | Chester Springs | Pennsylvania 19425

ISBN: 978-1-907593-20-8
4 6 8 10 9 7 5 3

A CIP record for this title is available from the British Library.

Cover design by Sin É Design
Internal design by Liberties Press
Printed in Ireland by Gemini International Ltd.

The publishers gratefully acknowledge
financial assistance from the Arts Council.

New and Selected Poems

Michael D. Higgins

Dedication

For Sabina, Alice Mary, John Peter, Michael, Daniel and
friends who have passed on, for those who remain, and for
those for whom I wait in anticipation

Acknowledgements

I would like to express my gratitude to Michael Treacy,
Niall Baneham, Noreen King and the invaluable editorial
assistance offered by Seán O'Keeffe

Note

Some of the poems included in this collection previously appeared
in *The Betrayal* (Salmon Publishing, 1990), *The Season of Fire*
(Brandon, 1993) and *An Arid Season* (New Island, 2004).

Contents

Foreword

Poetry in the broadest sense is probably our only way forward in destitute times. Perhaps it is unfortunate that we have to rely on such fragile antennae, but, at the moment, it is all we have got. At other turning points in history, science, philosophy, ethics or theology may have been sufficient; in the complicated and unpredictable times in which we live, art alone can provide the weak, yet indispensable, instrument wherewith to chart a way forward. It is almost as if the place we have reached in the tunnel we are burrowing is too narrow for grown adults to scramble through and we have to persuade children to ease their way through the opening, take the fall on the other side and then help us negotiate a passage for the rest.

'The poet', to use T. S. Eliot's phrase, 'is occupied with frontiers of consciousness beyond which words fail, though meanings still exist'. This is consciousness before and after it enters the idiom of rational thought. Mind is certainly an important part of the poetic act, but it is only one element. Heartwork is more essential. The finished form is filtered through consciousness, which is the place where many forces and energies meet to emerge as self-expression. The act of poetic creation opens the poet to worlds beyond the conscious mind. The poem is a use of words in whatever way is necessary to convey the new kind of reality which the poet experiences. The poet allows him or her self to be a filter for something beyond the self, something transcendent. This means that poetry is not the work of their own hands entirely; they leave themselves open to what is beyond the autonomous powers of their creative activity. Through the particular gifts of the poet, what is always entirely new, because it was never before articulated in history, becomes embedded in the familiar because it emerges in the form of a poem.

Understood in this way, poetry can be, and should be, a guide towards the future, an essential voice in the drama of creating a more habitable planet. If invited to undertake such a role, the danger is that poetry can become 'political', either in the sense that it produces politics or derives from politics. Although few believe that poetry should be 'political' in this sense, the discoveries it makes and the dimensions it reaches should be incorporated into the structures which are devised to achieve optimum quality of life for all inhabitants of our planet. In other words, poetry should certainly inform politics. Otherwise the pendulum swings into the other danger area, where poetry is siphoned into its own space and cultivated for its own sake, without connection with, or influence on, the way we live. Such limitations relegate it to the level of entertainment.

Michael D. Higgins exercises the ambiguous dexterity of being both poet and politician. But his poetry is not the fruit of his politics; it is the other way round. He takes time out from the hectic world of politics to make the difficult and dangerous journey to the depths of his own humanity and comes back with wisdom gleaned from that harrowing expedition.

> Your face haunts me, as do these memories;
> And all these things have been scraped
> In my heart,
> And I can never hope to forget
> What was, after all,
> A betrayal.

Everything we do in life is a betrayal of what is left undone. The politician betrays the poet; the teacher betrays the pioneering inventor. We cannot do everything we ought to do. No matter what good action we undertake someone in the world is neglected by our alternative attentiveness. And yet, as we move forward step by step, our carelessness is offset by our commitment to essential causes.

Michael D. has campaigned for human rights in Turkey, Western Sahara, Nicaragua, Chile, Gaza, The West Bank, Peru, El Salvador, Somalia. He has fought against dogmatic blueprints for our future whatever their provenance. 'Nothing is inevitable' and 'everything is possible' have been the liberating bumper stickers of his political campaigns.

These poems unearth the provenance of his subtle alignment with the poor and the weak in our universal society. His book is 'the salt of tears,' 'a deposit in memory of our sea beginnings' where 'is lodged the long sigh of all our time, lost in endless space.' These are womb poems, deep memories of the time and place where we were born. 'I've been born and once is enough./ You don't remember, but I remember,/ Once is enough'(T. S. Eliot again). Where and when we are born are less essential anecdotes: some years before the outbreak of the Second World War when Ireland entered 'An Arid Season'. However, despite that trauma 'The task lies in getting beyond that to the hope that solidarity and commitment brings.' Michael D. the politician has a way forward for the author of these poems. And a wonderful sense of humour alleviates the sometimes scarifying memories of childhood.

Above all this anthology of poems, collected over a lifetime of snatched breathing spaces, is homage to our most precious gift of language. It is exploration of meaning beyond the inevitable claptrap of politics and the normal currency of words. At a time when language loses meaning, when life becomes commodity, when values are lots at the auctioneers' disposal, our personal duty is to return to the source where the heart utters truth in stammering soliloquy, where

> The stuff of hope beckons.
> Out of the darkness

Abbot Patrick Hederman OSB
June 2011

11

I

Early Days

I was born in Confraternity City, Limerick, in 1941, but remember little of my early years. We left at the age of five. My father's pub, however, I do remember. My mother occasionally brought me in to see him standing behind the teak counter in his long apron. I recall the magic trapdoor that covered the cellar; somebody once fell down through it. Downstairs he bottled stout, and I recall his head emerging as he rolled barrels up the stairs. Around the pub itself were the snugs, cloister-like.

My father was the youngest of a family of ten children. As a boy he had been apprenticed to a grocer in Ennis. Thanks to the assistance of an Australian relative, he had got a chance his widowed mother could not give the older children. His eldest sister emigrated to Australia before he was born. The others had scattered; two of my aunts lived with my uncle on the small family farm from which he had come.

Only much later was I to know what my father's life had been like before those early years in Limerick. It was to be pieced together through a hundred fragments of conversation and a thousand chance encounters. My uncles had, with my father, fought in the War of Independence. When the Civil War came, he went with what he called the Republicans – or what Paddy Cooney would call the Irregulars. My uncles went with the Treaty side.

In those early years I remembered my mother straight-backed for the only period of my life. We were in the brief comfortable period of my parents' life – about eight years in all. As he had been arrested and detained to the end of the Civil War, my father had lost his job. He had also been harassed in County Clare in his home parish by those who, at that stage, would not speak after Mass to a

Republican. He left, and rented, and later bought, a pub. My mother, after her own mother's death, left her home in County Cork. She had known my father there in the 1920s – and had married him in 1937.

All four children – twin girls followed by two boys – were born in a space of four years, around my mother's fortieth birthday. This was a favourite topic with her. 'Marry before you're thirty or else don't marry at all', she would say. It was perhaps her second most depressing remark. The most depressing was: 'If I was starting again, it's into a convent I'd go.'

I remember her in her long fashionable leather coat pushing me along the Jamesboro Road in Limerick. Later, the coat was cut down for one of us to wear. My father had been told that I should have Guinness to build me up as a child: I recall being brought by him into the snug in another Limerick pub – Gussy O'Driscoll's. He also brought me into a billiard hall. These images are the ones I have of the period before the most traumatic event of my life.

One day, I woke to hear my mother crying. My father was attempting to rise out of bed but was unable to do so. The ambulance was coming, and we children were all bundled off to a neighbour. It was exciting, I recall. But I can still see my mother, out on the street looking after the ambulance, and crying.

'What is to happen to us?' she said. Every day she visited him. For weeks he was near death. Then he began to recover and we went to see him. We brought oranges and apples for him. The nuns always seemed to be talking to my mother about how difficult a man my father was. He was not a good patient.

All that time my father was ill, in 1946, my uncle and aunt visited him in hospital. On their way home, they would call on my mother and us children. They had concluded that my mother could not manage four children. Unmarried and childless, they persuaded her that, at least for a period, they would take my four-year-old brother and myself to live with them on the farm in County Clare. My mother was too 'soft' in her approach to the world, in their view. They had never completely approved of my parents' marriage.

On 15 August 1946, the Feast of the Assumption, they collected us in their 1938 black Ford motor car. I can remember only parts of the journey. I recall that we drove at dusk up through some fields to their home, which was a single-storey three-bedroomed farmhouse. The traditional large kitchen and one room were thatched, and one room was slated. This was to be my home for thirteen years.

I recall in particular the excitement of my aunt at having two young children coming to live with them. My brother John and I experienced all the sensations of the country. I learned how to milk a cow, burying my forehead against the udder, watching the milky foam rise against the rivets on the side of the galvanised bucket. I learned how to draw a calf, the legs appearing first from the cow. I learned to plough, holding the handles steady so as to break the earth evenly. I learned to sow turnips and knew the names of twenty different types of apple tree.

In time, we went to a small national school. In the single large room, the master, William Clune, taught the senior classes at one end, while at the other end, Miss Hastings taught the infants and juniors. At lunchtime, the schoolchildren would erupt out onto the hard-packed earth that constituted the playground, leaving Mr Clune and Miss Hastings to the ritual of setting out their lunch.

In the playground, the idea was to commit yourself to every scrumlike encounter. We all went barefoot in summer – not from necessity, but by choice. This enabled a kind of County Clare kung fu to develop in the skirmishes. Going home over the dusty gravelled road, we picked sugar beet which had fallen from lorries. Before crossing the fields, we stopped to look at the train bringing Mr O'Dea's beets to the factory. In the winter we brought turf, and on the wet days toasted bread in front of the school fire.

By now, my uncle was growing ill and had taken to bed. He was tended to by my aunt, who also had to care for her disabled sister. This sister slept behind a special wooden construction in a corner of the kitchen; she died within two years of us arriving at the house.

I recall her wake vividly. The good bedroom had been

reconstituted as a parlour, where the women were served port wine. In the barn, the men drank glasses of porter filled from large jugs. My aunt was laid out in the kitchen. The coffin, surrounded by candles, lay on a table. It is the smell of wax and wine that I recall. That and the fact that a man who was eating ham sandwiches was advancing towards one of our middle-aged female neighbours. We had been put in bed in the other room but got up again. We were excited because our father was due from Limerick.

He had been looking for work. His business, which had been in decline before his illness, was now gone. He had sold his house and was living with my mother and twin sisters in a rented house in Limerick. Whenever he came, he gave us money and sweets. Now we learned that he had decided to rent a grocery shop. We thought this was extremely exciting but the reality for him was very different. Rationing had come, and nobody could move their ration book to him. My father came on one occasion, and all he had to give me was a little badge from his coat.

We were brought to visit him and my mother and sisters about once a month. What I remember most is the chips. My mother could make chips, and my brother and I thought they were great. Then the shop failed, and my father, mother and sisters moved to a flat – the first of several. It was decades before apartments were invented. Auctioneers had not yet become estate agents, even if the odd bookmaker had become a turf accountant.

My father was now working as a barman – a job he was to have for less than a year. After that came the long searches for work. He got a job once, for a month in a shop in Nenagh. But things were getting worse. My mother now had her eyes set on a corporation house in a new estate in Rathbane in Limerick. She felt we could all be together if we had a 'proper' house. After a couple of years, a house was allocated to us, and my father wrote to us in County Clare to tell us the news.

Then, very suddenly, the aunt who had reared my brother and me died. She had a stroke while out in the field calling us. Immediately afterwards, my uncle persuaded my father to bring the rest of his family to County Clare. After all, the children would get the land. Thus, in the mid-1950s, we were all reunited.

One of my twin sisters joined my brothers and me at school. I recall going home one night from a neighbour's house and my sister holding my hand as we made our way in the dark up the narrow, hilly road. It was a good, and new, feeling.

The nineteen fifties was a hard time for us. The thatch was growing nettles, and it had holes in places. The broken windows were not repaired. My uncle was in bed most of the time. My mother was never happy in the country and missed the noise of the city. She clung to her dream of getting a house; she seemed to think that any effort in the house where we lived was a struggle against the tide. The other children knew of our condition and, occasionally, when passing us on their way home from school, shouted at us about our broken windows.

At that time, we listened to the wireless. (God bless John Kelly TD for keeping the word 'wireless' alive, even in Dáil debates.) Life in the nearby town of Newmarket-on-Fergus was typical of any village at that time. On Sunday the cars – not so many of them then – parked in front of the church and disgorged their passengers. At the side of the church wall were rings for tying the reins of horses which had drawn the (much more numerous) traps. The middle section of the church was mixed, with the men's aisle to the right and the women's confraternity and choir to the left. Upstairs were the men's and women's galleries. In the main gallery, the seats carried shining brass plates bearing the names of the donors. The front seat was occupied by the doctor and his family, the second by Mr and Mrs Hastings and their daughters.

Into these prominent seats every Sunday filed all the members of local notable families. I recall, when I was allowed go to the men's gallery, the looser relationship the gallery members had to the service, compared to the males in the main body of the church: the smells, the sweat from bodies mixed with dust from the kneeling forms, the caps on which one knee could be precariously balanced even if one did not get a seat.

After the sermon, the priest read the announcements. The postmaster was selling tickets for the parish annual pilgrimage to Knock. The electricity was coming, and everyone should take it. It had been offered before, and this would be the last time. The church year had as its high point the Eucharistic procession, when the Newmarket-on-Fergus Brass and Reed Band played. By now, Newmarket-on-Fergus had gone republican in the safe way; the only other occasion they played was for the passing through of de Valera on his way to Ennis. I recall the faces of the bandsmen and remember speculating as to whether their purple cheeks would burst or their eyes pop out.

The tension in the house was considerable. Years earlier, I had found in the drawer of a cupboard my uncle's blue shirt, and had been told not to ask about such things. I had been told too that the republicans were blackguards. But my father was one of them, and now we all shared the same living space.

My father made only one attempt to get a job after he came to County Clare. It was a job as a van driver. I went with him. 'What age are you?' the wholesaler asked. 'Fifties,' my father lied. 'Would you be able to move those doors?' asked the wholesaler, pointing to the great sliding doors on a huge van.

We went home. He was to never work again. But he did teach us to make shoes, to fish, and many other things. We were keeping fewer cattle now. I had in my earlier years gone at break of light to fairs in Sixmilebridge and elsewhere. We liked it: running ahead in turns to stop the cattle from going through gateways and byroads, occupying the best location we could, so that the buyers, mostly from Northern Ireland, would see the cattle. We were rewarded with lemonade and Marietta biscuits. Of course there was also the occasional dejected journey home with the cattle when the fair was bad.

But it was no hardship to bring them back. Each of them had a different personality, it seemed to us as children. I remember well when we were down to the last cow: a red one.

Few who have not been reared on a farm understand the

significance of these intimacies with animals, or indeed the disaster represented by the loss of a cow. It was the difference between freedom and complete dependence. When the cow dies, there is no surplus milk. You then have to rely on a neighbour for milk. I remember my mother, white-faced, looking into the ashes, poking them with a tongs as she waited for news from the barn that the red cow was dead. The smell from the barn confirmed the verdict. 'We were never short of milk,' she said slowly and quietly. Soon afterwards, sacks of potatoes arrived from the neighbours as a gift.

Knowing he was about to die, my uncle set to making a will. I remember the arrival of the solicitor. A small, curly-haired man, he looked, I recall, like an agitated sparrow. He was very cross at having to come from Ennis, and kept slapping the table and shouting: 'I must have quiet!' We were all sent outside while the pompous little man wrote the will.

It was only when my uncle died that we realised that he had left the farm to us children, not my father. It could not be sold. My father would have to rely on any rent he could get for it. That was a disaster. My sisters left for England to work in the railway stations in Manchester, who provided accommodation and a free rail ticket. Soon the letters with English money began arriving. For five years, my brother and I went to school in Ennis on our bicycles: nine and a half miles there and back every day.

It was now the mid-fifties. We listened to Radio Luxembourg on the new electric radio. I liked *Hancock's Half-hour* and we listened to matches.

Secondary school was the way out, I recall. By now my mother, bent in two from lifting pots on an open fire, her fingers cracked from pulling the pot hooks on the crane, saw her hopes for the future there. My father's health was failing. My brother and I got jobs in factories in Shannon: now we could pay the debts in the local shop. It would not be necessary to shuffle past, fearing the call from a generous man: 'Can you come here a minute . . . '

My father took to wandering the fields. His anger grew, and he was unbearable at times. My mother bore it well. My father I recall crying only twice in his life. Once was in hospital before he died. The other was when he had watched the two dogs who wandered the fields with him die in agony from strychnine poison which had been put down by a neighbour.

I decided that I had to leave. I had been offered the usual list after the Leaving. I nearly became a national teacher but my family did not have what was required for St Patrick's Training College in Drumcondra. At the end of the list of jobs was one as a clerical officer in the ESB in Galway. I went, having offered to send money home to my brother.

My brother now moved my parents to a two-roomed railway cottage. It had a slate roof and was dry. My mother felt that my father was very ill, and wrote to me. Soon he was in the General Hospital in Ennis. Not dying fast enough, he was to be transferred to St Joseph's, known by the saint's name – but in common parlance as the poorhouse. And I was to persuade him to go in. I did it. Quietly.

I went down a week later to see him. I walked into the main dining room, where he sat – a small, shrivelled man, reaching for a potato, peeling it with his thumbnail. It was me who had left him in, I thought, pushing him to Admissions in a wheelchair. In the hospital, he had broken an attendant's glasses. He had wanted to get out. The sister asked if I could pay for the glasses: the Social Welfare took so long.

My father being admitted often came back to me afterwards. I recall going out on the road at Ennis and hitching a lift back to Galway with tears in my eyes. Was I running away from my father? Within a year, the word came to me, at night, that he had died. He and the fellow republicans he had met in his last hospital had been betrayed by those who had stolen the dream of a free and independent Ireland. Now he need be angry no more.

We declined the sleveen republican offer of a military funeral. My sisters came from England; I came from Galway; we buried my father and then we scattered away. My mother got lifts to see him in the hospital and talked of it afterwards, of putting her hand under his head – which was the greatest softness for years between them that I had heard her talk of. I knew then she loved him in her own way. Less than five years later, she died too, slowly and painfully, from a throat illness. Within a few years, my brother would build his own house. She never got hers.

I was in Galway, had got a loan and gone to England, and was heading for university. My life would change. I was busy trying to survive, to escape. But is life not always like that? Is it not false to reconstruct a period from external events only? One's own biography has to be linked to history. Today there are those who are deeply hurt, so badly that they cannot see beyond their own pain. The task lies in getting beyond that to the hope that solidarity and commitment bring.

The betrayal

This man is seriously ill
the doctor had said a week before,
calling for a wheelchair.
It was
after they rang me
to come down
and persuade you
to go in
condemned to remember your eyes
as they met mine in that moment
before they wheeled you away.
It was one of my final tasks
to persuade you to go in,
a Judas chosen not by Apostles
but by others more broken;
and I was, in part,
relieved when they wheeled you from me,
down that corridor, confused,
without a backward glance.
And when I had done it,
I cried, out on the road,
hitching a lift to Galway and away
from the trouble of your
cantankerous old age
and rage too,
at all that had in recent years
befallen you.

All week I waited to visit you
but when I called, you had been moved

to where those dying too slowly
were sent,
a poorhouse, no longer known by that name,
but, in the liberated era of Lemass,
given a saint's name, 'St Joseph's'.
Was he Christ's father,
patron saint of the Worker,
the mad choice of some pietistic politician?
You never cared.

Nor did you speak too much.
You had broken an attendant's glasses,
the holy nurse told me,
when you were admitted.
Your father is a very difficult man,
as you must know. And Social Welfare is slow
and if you would pay for the glasses,
I would appreciate it.
It was 1964, just after optical benefit
was rejected by de Valera for poorer classes
in his Republic, who could not afford,
as he did
to travel to Zurich
for their regular tests and their
rimless glasses.

It was decades earlier
you had brought me to see him
pass through Newmarket-on-Fergus
as the brass and reed bank struck up,
cheeks red and distended to the point
where a child wondered whether
they would burst as they blew
their trombones.
The Sacred Heart Procession and de Valera,

you told me, were the only occasions
when their instruments were taken
from the rusting, galvanised shed
where they stored them in anticipation
of the requirements of Church and State.

Long before that, you had slept
in ditches and dug-outs,
prayed in terror at ambushes
with others who later debated
whether de Valera was lucky or brilliant
in getting the British to remember
that he was an American.
And that debate had not lasted long
in concentration camps in Newbridge
and the Curragh, where mattresses were burned,
as the gombeens decided that the new State
was a good thing,
even for business.

In the dining room of St Joseph's
the potatoes were left in the middle of the table,
in a dish, towards which
you and many other Republicans
stretched feeble hands that shook.
Your eyes were bent as you peeled
with the long thumbnail I had often watched
scrape a pattern on the leather you had toughened for our
    shoes.
Your eyes when you looked at me
were a thousand miles away,
now totally broken,
unlike those times even
of rejection, when you went at sixty
for jobs you never got,

too frail to load vans, or manage
the demands of selling.
And I remember
when you came back to me,
your regular companion on such occasions,
and said: 'They think that I'm too old
for the job. I said that I was fifty-eight
but they knew that I was past sixty.'

A body ready for transportation,
fit only for a coffin, that made you
too awkward
for death at home.
The shame of a coffin exit
through a window sent you here,
where my mother told me you asked
only for her to place her cool hand
under your neck.
And I was there when they asked
would they give you a Republican funeral,
in that month when you died,
between the end of the First Programme for Economic
    Expansion
and the Second.

I look at your photo now,
taken in the beginning of bad days,
with your surviving mates
in Limerick.
Your face haunts me, as do these memories;
and all these things have been scraped
in my heart,
and I can never hope to forget
what was, after all,
a betrayal.

Relatives Assisting

A room in the house
and a seat in the car to Mass,
that was the promise made in wills
to look after those
who did not travel,
but chose instead
to ride High Nelly bicycles to church
on Sundays, where they knelt
in the women's aisle, and listened
to visiting missioners thunder about
the sins of the flesh, and how
Queen Elizabeth had died,
rolled in a ball in agony, screaming
for the one True Church. It was too late,
of course, and it was a good feeling
for even a little while to be pure.
The Child of Mary medal was a consolation
and would travel with them
to the grave. And in the room guaranteed
you could 'prepare your black'
and save shillings from sales of egg and butter
for porter at your wake.
'Relatives Assisting',
they called you on the forms.
You had no acres, no lovers, no children,
but you had
what was more important,
a room in the house
and a seat in the car to Mass,
and in the meantime,
your High Nelly bicycle
and your prayers.

The Master

There was once an old master who was
very cold.
Each morning outside his school
he'd line them up,
Shine your shoes children,
be erect.
Shine your shoes or you will
gather faggots from ditches
for the school, for the parish, for
Jesus and the civil service.
Shine your shoes.

Inside the school awaiting the inspector
he'd stand little girls on desks
and lash their calves
until the weals showed
and the tears came.
Know your verbs or you're going
nowhere, he'd shout,
You'll be gathering faggots from
ditches
for the school, for the parish, for
Jesus and the civil service.
Learn your verbs.

At evening going home
the villagers would avoid his gaze.
Catching their eye, the master might
not even nod.
They always froze,
for he was a cold man.

At four his wife would say,
The master's home,
children, finish your tea.
Blessing himself, he would eat,
for he was a religious man,
but he would not speak.
His wife,
bearer of their children,
would occasionally whisper
The master's thinking.

In his room he would sink to his
knees and pray,
Oh Jesus, I've done all this for you.
I've brought order,
I've brought discipline,
for the school, for the parish and
for you Jesus,
and I've sent them to the civil service.
Send me a sign.

And thus it was that one evening
in a blue haze
to his room a lady came.

My Son asked me to come, she said,
for He was afraid of you Himself
and He told me to tell you —
for mothers must always bring
messages —
that He said it all on the Mount:
love everybody,
but particularly
love yourself.

The master jumped from his knees
and, tearing off his clothes,
laughed and ran from the room.
I've had a sign, he told his wife,
I've had a vision.

Running into the street, the
villagers heard the Master's
cries
I've had a sign,
I've had a vision.

He ran to the edge of a wood,
where they found him
embracing a tree.

At first they were timid
for they were, after all, his pupils
at one time or another.
And one of the braver threw a blanket over him,
saying, with a soothing repetition,
Yes, master, of course, master,
you've had a sign,
you've had a vision.

And they brought him to hospital,
where all he would say was
I've had a sign,
I've had a vision.

At first the villagers simply said
to each other, in pubs,
Imagine the master, of all people.
And then much later, in shops,

31

It could happen to any of us.

They visited him in hospital
and they brought him books
which he never read,
saying simply,
with a smile that shocked them,
I've had a sign,
I've had a vision.

And after a while the villagers were
happy to hear the news from the hospital.
They've allowed him to arrange the flowers on the altar,
isn't that nice, some said.
And in the hospital the matron watched with pleasure
as the master smiled,
the flowers in perfect taste arranged,
but shook her head as she heard him say,
I've had a sign,
I've had a vision.

And it was a Sunday ritual
that his wife and children would come
and he would smile at them and say,
I'll tell you a secret,
love everybody, but particularly
love yourself
that was my vision.
And it was on such an occasion
that his son burst out,
Father, fuck your vision,
stop this nonsense
and they'll let you out.

But the master looked at him and wept

and then he smiled and said,
Do not ask me to go back,
do not hurt yourself,
no, my son,
love everybody,
but particularly love yourself.
That was my vision.
His son wept and shook his young head
and in the village they concluded
that the master was indeed mad.

Requiem for a parish priest

He stands at the window,
the old parish priest with rheumy eyes.
His eyes catch the graveyard stones
as he holds his glass of sherry.
Later, after tea and scrambled eggs,
it will be port or brandy.

The *status anamarum* lies finished
on the mahogany table.
His hand trembles
as he thinks of God and souls.
How often had he spoken of such things
and on occasion lately,
but much more rarely,
of Jesus.

The book of homilies lies open.
Make it relevant, it said,
use images.
Life is like knitting a jumper:
if you drop a stitch
go back,
unravel and pick it up again.
Too trite.

And anyway he was too old for all this stuff,
of Jesus and knitting.
He sinks into the black leather chair
his sister bought
when he got his first parish.
The smell of leather still mingled
with tobacco and sherry.

Leaving Maynooth so long ago
he would have mocked
such a throne,
idealistic then
when things were simple
'twas easily known
when souls were won or lost,
when shepherds called the shots
and good sheep knew their place.

But was it not those halcyon days
of simple truth that ruined his life?
His housekeeper was the first to notice his doubt.
Afraid to speak, she hid the bottles,
bringing them away,
not putting them in the bin,
for discretion's sake.
And before that first visit to St Pat's
he foxed her with whiskey in hot water bottles.
It was the soul that needed warmth,
not his body,
he'd told himself.

He'd lasted through a lot
for days when he shared glasses of stout with reverential
    farmers,
who later mocked him when his words were slurred.
Their children, wide-eyed, eating Marietta biscuits,
wondered why the priest was strange
even if it was in the snug he sang
or wandered through sections of Canon Sheehan.

Always on the morning after
he would tremble as he thought of lifting the Host

or sweating as he struggled through the Communion.
His bishop advised him at first to rest
and later to pull himself together
as he gave him a remote parish.

He took to writing verse.
The soul is not a garden
but a parlour overcrowded
with bric-à-brac, he'd written.
It didn't work as his mind wandered
over memories of lost times,
forgotten friends
and a life lost
on truths too carelessly embraced.

He stayed alone while he was sober.
Some said, of course,
when they discussed such things in the parish,
as they did in hushed tones,
that he was holy,
that he was an ascetic.
The doctor's wife used that word,
for she was educated.
The older women said
that he was holy,
that he could cure baldness in children,
ringworm and warts.
The rumour was general.

The tears fill the eyes grown small
in a red area of facial flesh.
He turns away and a smile breaks.
That was what they all missed.
Was Christ's face not swollen in the Garden?
Had he not been reduced

to being a sorceror?
And did they not know then in their hearts
who suffered alone?
He would have his scrambled eggs
and after that a port
or perhaps a brandy,
and wait for them to call
about baldness in children,
ringworm and warts,
and maybe
in healing them all
he'd heal himself.

The death of the red cow

On horse-fly days she occasionally ran
but usually she ambled,
as she led home cows not as experienced
and skittish heifers too.

It was to her a child could be allocated
where the swish of a dirty tail
was the only danger.

Measuring her yield
against the rivets sinking under the foam
in the galvanised bucket,
a child's heart filled with love
as one's forehead pressed her udder
from which, even at five,
you knew how to remove *sciartáns.**

Most loyal of providers, you loved her,
and when the voices woke you at night,
you knew at once
that it was from her stall,
in what adults would like to call a barn,
that the commotion came.

They tried the nails on her hips
and buckets of gruel were brought
but, when you came,
the stench around her open mouth
told you
that the red cow was dying.

The lights of the vet's car
brought hope
but his words were short:
I'm sorry.

And you broke the news to your city mother,
who only said:
Milk was the one thing
We were never short of.

And on the following morning
the Burkes sent potatoes,
but life would now change utterly.

The separator's basin no longer needed
to be shone,
the steel discs disassembled,
and there would be no contest
as to who could last longest
turning the wheel.
There would be no more measures
of pints and quarts of her yield.

When the red cow died,
your time for fields was over,
and now there would be
the scattering
and the measures only
of escape
and your own life.

---

* *sciartán:* a blood-sucking maggot found on cows' udders.

Dark memories

Sitting in a dark room, she'd ask me
not to turn on the light,
that her tears might not be seen.
We'd know it was like that
for, earlier, she might have said,
If I was starting out again,
it's into a convent I'd have gone,
away from all the trouble.
Or she would have spoken
of lovely times in the shop, drinking
tea and eating Marietta biscuits,
or taking a walk with her little dog,
after playing the piano in the sitting-room
over the shop, where soldiers came
and bought more biscuits, when life
was easy in Liscarroll,
a garrison town; before my father
blew up railway lines and courted his way
into her affections.

She stood straight then, and, in a long leather coat,
after her mother died, she packed her case,
left and joined him a full decade after
the civil war. And she had loved him
in her way. Even when old Binchy placed a note
behind the counter in his shop
in Charleville, stating that when all this blackguardism
was over, there would be no jobs
for Republicans in his firm, or anywhere else,
for that matter.

Now bent and leaning towards the fire,
with blackened fingers holding the tongs,
she poked the coals; and we knew
it best to leave her with her sorrow
for her lost life, the house she'd lost,
the anxious days and nights,
and all that might have been.

We ran outside and brought in turf
and did our lessons and vowed that we would listen
to what she said, of cities where always
there were voices for company, and churches
close by, if never cheap.
We would listen to her story
and vow that, for her at least,
we, her children, would escape.

Against all certainty

There is something so easy about certainty.
In front of the shrine of St Jude,
the little white-haired lady looks anxious.
In the main aisle, the middle-aged man
in a grey suit and a beautiful, fresh pink face
looks certain.

It is, I suppose, something like
the difference between
Saving Certificates
and a Lotto ticket.

But I want her to win with St Jude,
at least share the jackpot,
and I wouldn't collapse if he
lost some of his Certificates.

Or is it that I envy his certainty?
Recalling times
leaving the intimate smell
of the confessional,
I bent my head in great relief;
forgiveness was certain.
And the sun shone with a blinding energy
in my eyes when I came out.
And the gravel sang to me
outside the church
under my foot.
Days of certainty.
And if it was not for the fact
that God did not call

people like us,
I might have loved to be
imparting certainty
in a sweaty box
for life.

The scruple is the maggot in the heart of certainty
that breaks the core
with its question.
Are you sure you can be certain
of anything
for which you should be forgiven?

A man came home from England
and, robbed on the boat
between Holyhead and the city
he never knew as capital,
felt he had been judged
for only an occasional Mass
in England,
punished to return
with a dirty shirt
and an empty pocket.

All us children heard him scream.
Or was it a cry?
For only the banshee cried
in our village.
And he tore at the roots of the furze,
saying he'd find the gold
that all the old ones missed.
And when they found him,
his face was scraped
as he rubbed his soil-filled nails
around his wild eyes.

He was never the same.
We children were told
not to ask questions.
And he never again was able
to go home alone
from games of forty-five.

But, passing up the hill
where on the old road
the bushes threatened to make a canopy,
one's eyes could not avoid
the shrine stone with its edge of moss
upon which he knelt
and prayed for forgiveness.

Was it not a holy stone?
And if the shift of guilty gravel
was not in doubt,
should one not kneel
not only for him
but for oneself?

The soil under his nails,
and yours,
was poison.
To clean one's nails in church
was sacrilege
that could never be told
in a wooden box
of sweat and a small curtain.
There could never be certainty again.

And if one looks
and hopes the white-haired lady

wins the jackpot with a little help
from St Jude,
and if one gazes at the pink face
of the man more certain,
is it not a glance in a terrible mirror
where those more certain
can smile for ever?

And then if tears are now allowed
the grown person
that was the child,
is it not better
to be uncertain, to have the scruple
and throw away the apple
that was certainty?

For now you see them both
that cannot see each other,
who kneel,
and the pain of the heart is real,
and where there was gravel
there is the uncertainty
of love
that needs the polish
of a restless wonder,
that gives those glimmers,
even, on occasions,
that confirms
we make our own uncertain magic.

Sunday ceremonies in Clare

From the moment
of the beguiling words,
assisted with a promise
not to be taken seriously,
to the discovery
of a secret place
of hazel,
floored with damp mosses
and threaded only with an occasional
briar,
it was unstoppable.

The stretch of limbs
among the thorns
brought shrieks of pain,
defeated
by the pleasure
of the pounding
when it came,
all over in a moment.

Nor was there any lingering
as the betraying foliage
was dusted
from the crumpled clothes
that carried
the secret
of this roadside shrine,
a secret made
between the morning pitch and toss
behind the alley
and the encounter

with Sunday afternoon snores,
disturbed only
by a score on the radio
from Croke Park,
this miracle
occurred.

Later, passing the spot
on one's way to Benediction,
no guilt
assaulted the senses,
rather,
a throbbing recall of memory.

But when the monstrance rose
above the heads
and wonder came
as to whether
that yawn not stifled
would lock your jaw
for ever
at a sacrilege,
the black clouds threatened.

On the return home,
the thought rankled,
as the place was passed
where the miracle of discovery
took place,
all rain and mud
and rotting leaves.
No shrine intact.

It would take courage
to decide

that true belief
does not require
a choice between
the shrines
of differing magic.

In Croke Park,
life was easier.
Kerry defeated Dublin.

Brothers

When we set out together to find
our new home,
I suspect
we cared less
for the broken heart of our mother
who had let us go
than for the wonder
of the journey
in a black Ford Eight
through fields
at twilight.

It is that wonder
that brings me back
to the age of five,
not any great grief
I should have felt
or tears I should have shed.

And then, we were
together,
a source of curiosity,
a legacy from tragedy
that had given a childless pair,
an uncle and an aunt,
two instant children,
brothers
so alike
we could be twins.
That's what they said.
We did not find

Michael D. Higgins

the bonding
of such words
a burden.

We stood together in photographs.
Our teeth defined
a hidden difference
and, on our city visits,
both wearing boots
for the lasting,
not shoes,
which we were told by our mother
were the mark
of civilisation
and the city,
our Communion suits, chosen
for next year's wear,
the sleeves
played with our knuckles,
another country sign
that made her sad.

At night, we shared a prayer
in a room
demoted from a parlour
to being the sleeping place
of aunt and child,
of uncle and child,
the parlour now the space
of what had once been
a four-poster bed,
a sofa and sister bed,
a well-sprung inheritance of iron,
replete with tick and bolster.
We learned those country words,

the rites of night
and intimacy.

Their shaking preceding our prayers,
'Matthew, Mark, Luke and John,
bless this bed that I lie on.'
Evangelists.
I learned the word
and thought of bells
and books
and quills
and long grey beards.

I placed them nightly
on the missing poles
of the bed, mutilated
without its postered canopy,
acquired from the scattering
of a half-great local house.

And little things were made
for the little men
who would one day be sure
to be a great help
when needed in hayfields
and the bog
or in the wet brown drills
of tillage.

You were better at all these
practical tests
of strength
and judgement too.
For me, the image of escape
distracted

from the tasks of place.
The books I loved
were instruments
for the breaking of the bars
and a run
towards the light
and a new life
back
in the city.

At times, on the bar of a bike,
I vowed
to bring you
where I presumed
you wished to go.

It was through pain
I realised
that our journeys
would be separate,
alone,
requiring different skills.

And I sought my brother
in a hundred others
for whom
my heart warmed
at shared
hopes
and fears.

Every embrace a compensation
for the lost moments
of feelings
buried beneath

the boulders
of other expectations
of duty
and respectability,
of fear
and dust
and sweat
and a life reduced
to rehearsal
for the decency in death
that was the legacy
of our family.

Back from the tomb,
Christ saw brothers
everywhere.
The stone rolled back,
he never returned
home
but embraced every stranger,
brothers all,
in the light,
out of the dark.

Katie's song

It is a story buried
beneath the clay of lost
intimacies,
a time sealed,
made safe from disturbance,
and a label that warns
of the danger in opening
the moulding jar
of memory.

And yet I see her,
legs stout,
apart,
trying to snatch private time
for woman business,
for us the source
of wonderment
but, much more,
the threat and origin
of an averted gaze
that could never be
corrected.

Oh Katie, I remember
when your writing carried a flourish
and the lightness returned
to your fingers
as you smiled the magic
the school books you covered,
satchelled ambassadors
'twixt home and school,
our steps to the future.

Your fantasy
compensation
for a life
of lesser things.
Oh Katie, I would sing your song
if now I could recover
more
than your moments
of intimacy
and fantasy,
two threads that did not make
alone
the garment of your life.

On a sometime Sunday,
I recall
your playing with magic words.
You dressed yourself
with such unusual care
that the violence of my question
as to where you might be going
did not dislodge you from your dream.
You were not going to any haggard
that afternoon.
You were, instead, intent on strolling
in a pleasure garden
and you told us you had an appointment.
We, whose thoughtless demands
defined
your every action,
could not understand.

And, when you died,
after calling us for an hour,
your summons from the fields

Michael D. Higgins

not heeded
nor perceived,
your anxious tones,
faded,
alone,
at a distance
from children not your own,
moved to an unbearable anxiety.

Oh Katie, I am making my way
along a lane of hazel.
I am stretching
for the fire of the senses
that will bring me back
to where I can stand still and shiver
and weep
at all the love
you earned
never paid
by a child afraid,
in iceberg times,
to throw his arms around
the plump frame
of the maker
of his bread
and magic.

My mother married my father in Mount Melleray in 1937

Those photos were the most precious
from before.
She in slight profile,
her best side,
he fresh and determined,
A strong face, they said.
She wore her leather coat
for the going away
and he a blue-grey jacket,
in its lapel a badge
given as a gift
among many blessings
by the monk who performed the ceremony.

My mother married my father in Mount Melleray in 1937.

Why should we not weep
and make the salt
for other tears
that teach to grieve
and source the long sigh
that breaks
out of breath shaken
from the spirit
that trembles in its search
for truth.

The remembered humiliation,
the sharing of another's loss,
suggest a press of tears

that is too far from the heart,
distant from the source
that might connect the long sigh
to the wound deep
in interrupted breath.
I weep for the lost child
not allowed by times,
made adult too soon
to gaze at joy exchanged,
hear words bartered
in laughter.
It is the little things
that make a resonance
for certain
in oblique constancy
lodged in creviced memory.
They hold on
and blossom.

My mother married my father in Mount Melleray in 1937.

On the side of a stony mill
my father,
going away again,
an exotic visitor,
tells me he will walk the remaining mile alone
to a bus that will pause in front of the familiar
withering cabbage plants in bundles,
forks and rakes in pristine cleanliness.
As we turn from each other,
I place my frail hope
in his surviving energy.
From the warmth of his jacket lapel
he takes a badge
worn since his marriage.

My mother married my father in Mount Melleray in 1937.

It is an old indented badge
moulded for the pushing through
and the anchoring,
not temporary,
image enamelled
of a cross and hand
with reds and greens I cannot now distribute,
sign of a confraternity,
a special membership,
something stubborn,
intimate,
that had migrated with him
in his despair.

From lapel of once-sturdy jacket
in fashion,
chosen for discretion in celebration,
to the familiar coat
of frayed intimacies
now worn for warmth
in the necessity of his visit
to us his children
that he had already half-lost,
its leathered cuffs asserting
a dignity of craft,
perhaps a prudence,
he takes it.

My mother married my father in Mount Melleray in 1937.

No coins left, nothing to give,
he takes it from his coat,

the badge more precious,
upon which my eyes had feasted
in his proximity.
He offers this gift in a hand I never kissed.
I kept it with me
and lost it in my own migrations.
When I remember now
this sacred little thing,
I want to grieve for him
and let his anger go,
and my childish shame.

My mother married my father in Mount Melleray in 1937.

I kept this secret gift
of my father
in the space shared
between us.
In a world of shortening time,
why is it not allowed to remember?
Why is it required to forego
small and sacred moments,
scarce and precious things,
from the spaces between
those iceberg times of forbidden touch,
the slightest sign of tears
and love?

My mother married my father in Mount Melleray in 1937.

Even through grief,
the healing is uncertain.
For all belief is thin belief
but little things can lodge
on a fragile surface.

Create a boundless aura
that enables the memory
to make a miracle.

My mother married my father in Mount Melleray in 1937.

The ass

I recall the soft velvet of his ears,
as he bent in habit
for the winkers,
the resignation too of his
taking the bit
past the surrender of his yellow teeth.

The cross upon his back conferred
no sacred status,
more a reminder of a burden carried,
nor did it guarantee
the paring of his hooves.

The head of an ass,
the warm udder of a cow,
the arrogant snort of a horse,
the exhausted pant of a dog,
the sharp cuts of a green fern,
the precarious blue of a bog iris,
the wonder of stranded eels,
the rush of water in gully and ditch.
What is it of these images that makes them endure
past a time of catastrophe,
the slow death of a house
where the thatch has given in?
It is a special intimacy perhaps,
allowed in fields,
that lodges them as seed
in memory.

On those rare occasions when he broke
from trot to gallop,

I soared with him past order,
before the tug on the reins.
And I never hurried at the untackling,
nor did I begrudge him
his freedom recovered.

More than an image lost
it is a companion
I seek
to recover.

Horseshoe

Out of proportion,
in the half-darkness,
the blows fall,
making sparks
from the molten magic.

Earth, fire and water
combine in the strike
of hammer on iron,
to make a shape
that arrives glowing,
held to the light,
only needing the space for nails,
a shining creation
that makes the badge of another's service.

On to the hoof the nails are driven
with certainty.
The rasp is last,
making smooth the transition to work
with winkers and chains.
The horse beats the road tenderly,
and who could decide
if it were music
or just a sign
of a life made useful?

And at the end on grass,
no new miracle
of the dark or sweat
is needed to make a shape

beyond the use of man.
The horse snorts,
in a brief freedom,
at one with earth and stone;
his hooves feel the freedom earned,
unshod,
after a life prescribed.

Too close to the ground

Too close to the ground,
our gaze was downwards
at the wet drill,
at the hooves of cattle,
eyes raised only to their backs,
driven before us to fairs,
where we competed for mute subjection.

Too close to the ground
for sunsets,
and landlord seasons,
making the sounds horses knew,
for the pulling of the plough
was a man's work.
Women making sounds
for ducks and geese,
that was our lot for language.

The gaze was never upwards.
To the sun we were indifferent,
at its going up and coming down
others marvelled.

Our children's children
talk of scenery
and the body
and the sea.
Too late for us.

Too close to the ground,
there were so many of us,

and we heard that some
in Africa, after the toil of day,
forgot the heat and in the cool of night
took signs from Sirius
and colours of lilac and orange
and black with shards of gold.

Heart and head are needed
in the raising of the head to the sun.
And in that action our world moans.
Waiting to be born, it cries out,
and we are reminded
that we make our own hope and history.

Inadequacy

To be near,
to be close,
to hold,
to touch,
to care,
to lie against,
in iceberg times.

Enough,
for the breaking of a heart

that asked,
mutely,

about sufficiency
of love.

One's own story

Our own story must always be lonely,
and when we pray from fear,
it must be a mumble,
out of some terror,
instilled,
a cry of the wounded,
without much hope of healing.

But if the truth be told,
our own story
brightens in the light of other stories,
older stories that glimmer,
lost in a long tail
of time.

We need these scraps
made luminous
to relieve the darkness
of our fall
from the imagined divine
towards that space
where the occasional sparkle
of the human
remains a prospect,
in the still space
of our loneliness,
as we pray
for the gift of love.

In memory deposit

A man falling back in bed,
a woman crying,
and we dressed for a journey.
How much is left in memory deposit,
of that great tearing,
of that great loss,
of a great separation,
and the opening of a great tear,
in the remnants of a family,
dragged down by circumstance?

As we headed into exile,
the wonder of the new made personal
prevailed,
would hold until the time came
for a great loss,
such a separation
as would make
a wound deposit
in memory.

Of sons and fathers

Is it the fate of sons to become their fathers,
shadow selves,
rejected?
That unavoidable destiny
beckons.
In the erosion of flesh,
it makes no allowance
for rejections
in the flush of youthful energy.
Too late for the anxiety
of a recovered love,
the memories haunt
and the dark guilt corrodes
at the realisation
of an irrefutable defeat.

Of sons and mothers

It may be the fate of sons
to become their fathers:
a terrible truth
best not avoided,
regret allowed.

But I am becoming my mother:
she has called me back,
she has reminded me
of that early wound.

They say you are like your father,
and I, a traitor, early
required the qualification,
not in every way of course.

Words of failure,
failed words,
failed fathers,
failed mothers,
failed son,
and an enduring memory.

The poisoning

Is it the fate of sons
to become their father
and in that fate,
unavoidable,
recover
in moments lit by the senses
a memory
of grief and loss?

When now I look and gaze
at black and brown and great white chest
at amber-dotted eyes and head
of my great friend,
who placed his total trust
in us who watched
his racing quest to catch
a scent of stranger or elusive fox,
and when time has robbed us
of our time together, I recall
an older story that will not, should not, die.

And it is no melancholy now
in memory I impose, my father,
on your response.
I respect your anger
as an act of cruelty
born out of a neighbour's spite,
know the abuse of such proximity
as authored this act
that left two dogs,
sharers of your intimacy,

writing in an agony
before a death
that sparked anew
a great despair
at all that you had lost.

And now for me at a distance,
in a strange space,
lectures on community ring hollow,
invocations to cooperation
make a dead echo,
insufficient for the erasing
from memory
of this terrible act.
This stuff of rural intimacies
should never be forgotten.

True grief requires that truth be told,
making way in time, who knows,
for such an amnesty among neighbours
as would make a truce in space and time
where proximity offers no choice,
suggests instead a lying amnesia
to hide a neighbourly violence.

For, if the truth be told,
I must recall
that it was in the autumn years of your hopeless life,
across the fields you did not own
but yet had made familiar,
you walked in silence.
Alone with you,
they ran past furze bushes
that in another time
you sought to clear,

and, in much later years,
past my escape to lecture halls,
I saw you in Clym Yeobright,
bent to the side of a hill,
tearing roots to make a clearance
that would not last.

And for a moment now in memory,
I must become my father,
recall that on the day he returned
there was no sign of tears,
but anger on his face.

His dogs had died.
And why should the writhing and the turning,
the moaning
in a slow death,
from a neighbour's poison,
be hidden?
Such is the stuff of rural intimacies,
never to be forgotten.

Now sinks the sun in burning red,
and comes the night with shadows dark.
The night is long and I, afraid,
remember,
and put a question now in fear:
is it the fate of sons
to become their father,
and do old wounds reopen when
space and time make even
the crippling ends of life,
as memory tears the cover
of those wounds that will not heal?

The ruin

Surrendered to ivy and ash,
stone and lime defeated
by the mud floors yield
in alien growth
after the human feet no longer
beat their daily rhythms
with barefoot sounds and kneeling prayers,
the old house back in nature's grip
in neighbourly accounts
becomes a ruin.

And in the orchard adjacent,
once called a pleasure garden,
moss-laden, the fallen tree
holds its life for a while,
touching the earth through brambles,
gone with the blossoms white and pink,
the early promise of apples,
some for the gathering,
others strewn in disarray,
for all the surrounding life,
half-lost in nettles, weeds and grasses,
united in their fragile vulnerability
to the violence of chance and a cruel brevity
that robs them of renewal
in a new season.

Yet house and garden out of season
are making a new beginning
in their becoming
a ruin.

II

Of Rural Realities

After the second Mass in Newmarket-on-Fergus, the congregation were divided between the smell of fresh bread from Cremins bakery and a rush for the papers sold from the front room and kitchen of a house on the Weaver's Road. It was pronounced 'Wavers Road'.

On the other side of the road stood the handball alley, lesser child in the pantheon of the GAA, and frequented by those from the cottages, and the curious, such as myself. Behind such a place, pitch and toss occasionally took place; it was not unrelated to the commencement of Holy Hour in the taverns down the road.

It was on such a Sunday occasion that I heard the word 'poet' perhaps for the first time. It was unfortunately used in a somewhat pejorative sense to refer to a man with long hair who lived alone. It was not some comparison with Yeats which drew the term upon this man, but his perceived personal eccentricity and the rather obvious fact that the rural water schemes had not yet reached his house.

From my mother, in particular, I acquired a love of books. I recall her telling me how she waited with excitement for the news from O'Mahony's bookshop in Limerick that the latest Annie M. P. Smithson book was in. My brother and I were also in a house that valued literacy, and our uncle and aunt pressed us to practise by reading the headlines on the papers. When we went to school, in my case at the age of nearly seven, this interest in reading was encouraged by an exceptional teacher, William Clune, brother of executed Volunteer Conor Clune.

Prose was in fashion, however, and it would be much later that I would encounter Patrick Kavanagh's work, for example. When I did, I believe it was 'Pegasus' that I read first; it was very much later that I read the optimistic 'My room', which had been written much earlier. Very much later, I came to see the varied spiritualities of earth and city that were reflected in Patrick Kavanagh's work: the consciousness of the experience of a migrant unsuccessful twice over, insofar as he stayed too long with the wet drills and left his move to the city too late.

The sense memory that informed my own poems reflects a positive experience at one level. I was, during my childhood in County Clare, learning all the tasks necessary for existence on a small farm. I watched for the gelatin hooves of the calf, and learnt to pull at the right time when a cow was calving. I watched the milk foam up from the rivets of a galvanised bucket and learned to avert my face from the lashing, and dirty, tail of a skittish heifer.

I was excited too by the range of equipment in the yard: pulpers, harrows, and the intricate assembly and disassembly of the separator, on which my brother and I took turns.

I had, however, no unqualified pleasure in all this. There were always jobs to be done – even ones which would, later, imperil the Sunday Western in Murray's Picture House in Newmarket.

My thoughts were an escape, and all my experience in education facilitated that grand aim. There was, too, the introduction of all the uncertainty of illness and insecurity, and the price that was required in terms of the suspension of the space of being young.

The education itself cast a shadow on my appreciation of poets. The verses had to be learned for examination success at secondary school level, and something called 'appreciation' had to be developed. It seems to me, in retrospect, that this was an exercise akin to gutting fish: necessary, distasteful, but requiring skill. The poets listed were reduced and domesticated, by which I mean made safe for dissection.

The living poets I would read later, and admire, had the capacity to be subversive, prove wrong the accepted myths, lay bare ignorance, intolerance; above all, see the irony of polite images that masked a vicious if unconscious hate or moral cowardice. I recall being moved by Austin Clarke's poem on the funeral of Ireland's first president, Douglas Hyde, 'Burial of an Irish President', with its accusatory lines that excoriated those hidden round the corner of a president's funeral service.

Tall hat in hand, dreading
Our Father in English. Better
Not hear that 'which' for 'who'
And risk eternal doom.

Following secondary school, where the curricular murder of Tennyson, Arnold and, above all, the Irish poets was more than compensated for by the loving, vigorous presentation of Shakespeare by Canon Maxwell – the scarlet lining of the flaps of his soutane flashing in all directions as he moved from being Shylock to Iago or Bassanio. The late Martin Kirwan longed to teach Anglo-Irish literature from a revisionist perspective, but settled for De Quincey.

After the Leaving Certificate, I headed for a factory job, like young people at that time. Few went to university then, and the teacher's children aimed for the training college. Following the 'Guide to Careers' in the *Irish Independent*, the ESB was the last semi-state body to which I had applied. I was offered a Grade VII clerical officer job in Newtownsmith. I did not know if such a place was even in the city, and thus I came to Galway city.

My movement to Galway seems to have been irreversible. From being a migrant entering the city, I have become a city person remembering rural intimacies. I did not long for a return to rural poverty, even if I held in my heart a love for animals and an unquenchable regard for the texture of rural life that would never fade.

As a young academic, influenced by Raymond Williams in particular, I rejected the 'pseudo pastoral' and the forced invention of community that was being discovered in the midst of conflict. I saw in the abuse of tradition and ruralism the face of reaction, a reaction that saw the city as the location of sin and lost virtue, and the country as a divine project – all this in a country that had expelled a quarter of a million people to the city (and mostly cities abroad) in the six years between 1955 and 1960 alone.

I had also come to see the importance of Sean O'Casey's statement that poverty was like a disease of the bones. Once there, it never leaves you. The awareness of that fact, the sensibility it makes possible, enabled O'Casey to see the unnecessary violence moved to the heart of a city that was deeply humanist in its instincts and humour.

It was in the city that Sabina and I made our lives, while staying in touch with her rural links and, to a lesser extent, mine. It was in the city that we would, as a young couple, meet institutional challenges, such as the arrangements for our children's education. For me, the arrival and maturing of my own children offered the challenge of transcending certain aspects of my remembered life and trying to be open to the new wonderment of our family's life.

Sense memory

The sense memory, stored,
waits for a new function,
kicking an old can,
the child admonished
by an amnesiac authority
that curtails his wonder,
forgets it had a function once.
The child gives it a new life
with string
or a kick.

The pouched sense memory,
thrown in to make a line,
waits for the spirit surge,
to give it new life
with a sigh
or a kick.
Without the benefit of authority.

The Inter

for Alice Mary

Watching you prepare for the Inter,
my daughter,
I see in the chaos of your room
a bird
scratching its nest into shape
and, through your door,
as between branches broken
with violence,
come my words
that startle.

What value
my distraction
from your task?
Yours was the task of shaping,
making your own order
in the chaos of others' demands.

Oh, I would that I had come
with a whisper,
edged one twig towards where you saw it.
But I am burdened with
a catalogue
of prefabricated designs,
ugly, efficient and guaranteed
to do the job.

When I come again
I will bring silence,
but know,

even in its noise,
it was love that informed my bad choice.

Move your twigs
into the pattern that suits
your moment
and, not from a distance
I hope,
I will look and wonder
at whatever shape
my love rests upon.

The age of flowers

My child-woman daughter
has been given a gift of flowers
but she wants to gather balloons.

White and red, gold and blue,
they float above her bent head.
Her thin fingers,
as she disentangles their gaiety
from the anchor of a chair,
move with frenzy.

When my irritation shows,
she anticipates the suggestion
that it is past the age of balloons,
that the age of flowers is a new season.

They are for the boys, she says,
seeking refuge in the collective
that is the child's brief allowance
from the tyranny of a life
where balloons must not be mixed with flowers.

Oh, my daughter, if you only knew
what pain I give myself,
to reflect and think
that I have been part
of the destruction of a child's wonder.

Carry flowers, balloons, blow whistles,
laugh and jump,
my woman-child daughter.

Break every binding string.
Stretch every sense.
Break every restriction
of those impulses without reflection,
that make the random utterances
of the day-release prisoner
of repression
that is your father.

Stargazer

for Mary Coyne

She stands,
supported by her stick,
in front of the gilt mirror
her husband bought
in a mad moment
after selling the calves in Claremorris,
in the first year of their marriage.

Neck stretched back,
she drops the lotion
in her one good eye.
The tears come,
and she remembers,
in her solitary kitchen,
times when she stretched her neck back
to show the stars to her seven children.

Uranus, Mars, Venus and the Milky Way
in the canopy over Claremorris:
she had traced them all
with her bright bride's eyes.

The tears come from her one good eye
for her scattered children
and her children's children,
seed of her seed.
The range is cold that once was warm.
On it she rests her hand
and remembers
times when, pressing her forehead

against the warm udder of a cow,
reluctant milk-giver,
she told them stories from Dickens,
of Ham and Twist.
And always they would say,
But tonight, will you show us the stars?

She stretches back again
to drop the lotion in her one good eye.
Alone, she steadies herself
and cranes her neck.
The darkness comes as the drops fall
on her one good eye.
And through the mist of tears,
she sees the empty kitchen.

There is nobody to ask now for the stars.
There is only silence,
and the memories of a world emptied of people,
of feeling.
She straightens in front of the gilt mirror
and wipes the tears from her face,
lined with a thousand stories.
Sleep was but a dark night,
and death a journey to the stars.

Mother of mothers,
stargazer,
dust of dust,
tonight, you say,
you do not need your one good eye
to read the signs of sky by night.
To read alone was all you asked,
be told of distant things.

Michael D. Higgins

Go out tonight,
stargazer,
and plot your journey home.

The delivery

I have delivered my children
to school
in the half-grey light.
Always
the half-grey light
reminds me
of anxious arrivals,
temporary releases,
hurried half-kisses,
furtively offered,
sufficient for that time
of the offering up.

Leaving,
I question my complicity.
Blind faith no longer
moves me.
I am the deliverer
of what were my children
to the Chapel of Fear,
for sacrifice.
I weep full tears,
alone.

The collecting

As my eyes peel the playground,
I am distracted by sounds that are chaotic
celebrations of release.
The harness of a satchel
is being tossed
with a disrespect
hard-earned.

The bag, discarded,
is placed in perspective
by an involuntary kick
from a stranger
who had not invested it
with the intimacies
of welts and warm shoulders.
It is the peopled yard
that attracts
the backward glance.

The classrooms, abandoned,
linger in empty silence
until morning,
when the breath of authority
will, again, define
their arbitrary purpose.

Their long shadow
captures the first words:
'I've a pile of homework.'

We drive on homewards
with the wedge of school between us.

The death of Mary Doyle

She knew that there was thunder
in the air
from the sulphur
she had come to know.
All day she had waited
for a visitor
to read the letter
from her daughter,
the nun,
who had written
earlier that week
from Africa.

Moving her hand along the handle
of her stick,
she sighs at all the stories
she has ready
of the older people
who had gone before her,
farmed these stony acres.

She talked too much,
she thought,
in recent times,
and then it all came clear
in silence.
She would go to the barn.
She loved it there,
where all seemed warm
and intimate too.
Taking her stick,
she stumbles

out the door
and pushes through the yard,
undisturbed
by green pools
of urine
and dung,
damp under her feet.

And it is the dryness
of the barn,
its thousand smells,
a shrine
that welcomes her.
In recent years, she'd come to know
a strange fire that sparks
from the embers
not lit from desire
but intimacies
stored
from days and nights
spent here
in better times
and all the laughter that filled this place.

Leaning towards the bin,
the smell of meal moulded
stirs the memory,
and pictures come
of hens and cheerful chatter,
the stickiness of new-born calves,
gelatin-heeled,
unsteady,
needing the pull of both hands
to stand,
wobbling,

waiting for the rack lick
of a cow's tongue
that was, with laughter,
invoked
to describe the quiff
of her first son's hair.

The colours of all the feathers
in a hundred nests
warm her heart,
which fills
as she tries to feel
the rounded shapes
finger-poked for eggs
in the bride years of her marriage.
Slowly rising, the warmth
moves from her fingers
through her body,
shapeless from the birth
of seven children.

Exploding through her head,
the thousand pieces,
gathered
in sense memory,
overwhelm.

She falls towards the crib
where the wood,
polished
by the neck of an itchy cow,
is marble smooth and warm
but offers no grip.

Lying tumbled in the rank hay,

she laughs
and still the colours come
of gold and amber,
of green gone brown.
She had it all.

The limber shoot
was browned by a season
that ran its course.
That rich gold head of grain
would break the stalk
in times of storm
or broken weather;
but, more often,

the stooking and the binding
intervened
between the time of fields
and the predictable
breaking
of the threshing.

She was an old sheaf
cut loose from binding,
all seed taken,
only the dried stalks
ready
for the bedding
of all the life
that heated with their breath
this barn.

They found her
pitched forward
among the hay

and screamed
when they saw the youth
of the smile
that covered all her face.
Her stick abandoned,
she held in each hand
straw and feathers.
They would have to clean her up
for the laying-out.

They did not speak
to each other
or the neighbours
of where they found her
and, at the laying-out,
a holy woman
with glazed eyes
claimed
she heard a crowd
of angels
come to bring her up,
inevitably,
to heaven.

It was not angels that sang her home
but cows and calves
and ducks and hens,
and they gave her colours
for her head,
and voices too,
and smiles and smells,
and the touch of love.

Not long after,
they decided

that it was better
to knock the barn.
It was upsetting,
particularly
to the holy woman,
who said
it held memories
that disturbed her
of that day
when Mary Doyle
went out to the barn
to die.

The Raft

The broken wood has drifted
on to the lonely beach they visit.
In collusion
they have made this space,
between moments stolen
from a life prescribed.

The materials discarded beckon,
have drifted
from a narrow function,
carry traces of their past.

A child envisages a raft
made from the useless flotsam,
in such time as may be allowed,
on which to embark upon a journey
for which there is no map.
He asks a preliminary question.
His father tells him
it is time to go home.

The shared moment is over.
Turning their backs to the sea,
they drive
away from wonder,
father and son
in silence.

On the shore, the broken bits remain,
waiting for the sea,
to make its new demands.

At night the child dreams
of a raft rising and falling
with the waves.
In sleep he visits again
the lonely beach,
and vows to make a return,
to try again.

His father turns out the light.

Meeting

Beneath
the blackness of a bog
reduced to soup,
beyond
the side of a mountain
made bare,
lies an old violence
against nature.
Sustained with a sneer,
hushed with a cuteness
that offers solidarity
in the covert greed
of gombeen mutterings.

You are right to make your demand.
Do what you like with it,
as your fathers did before you.
those few inches of soil
are all you have.
Who are all these strangers?
Are we not here for generations?
He had them now;
he could let go.
Banging the side of a car
with an ash plant
was the best way
to drive the cattle,
as your fathers did before you.
He was sucking diesel.

Hard-faced and cold,
he smiled at his own words.

> They resonated.
> He knew he had them.
> *Fuck the ecology,*
> they roared.
>
> Going home, he felt certain
> they would be his for ever.

On making the Three Decades

for Alice Mary

Time will never make a boundary that could contain,
nor space enclose,
those moments you turned to gold
with a light that will always be your own.

It is your special gift
to see the need for joy,
to muster a courage
so far beyond the ordinary,
to make of friendship
something sacred,
and feel the need to break the silences
that mask oppression.

These are no ordinary achievements.

We who were blessed with your presence
did not measure it in time
or confine it to any space,
nor do we now
put boundaries of time or space
on all we wish for you.

May that which you never measured
come back to you in love.

May the friendships you cherish multiply,
and we are grateful
for all those moments of dark and light you shared
and placed in our indelible memory.

Michael D. Higgins

May you never be alone
in what you seek,
and may you live to see the decades brighten again with hope,
beyond the darkness of war.

And when spirits lift
behind banners
in all those decades to come,
it is a source of the greatest joy to know
that you will be there,
and in the quiet times too,
plotting even greater things
for all humanity in ceaseless celebration.

After-Mass meeting

He has chosen his spot
in the place held
by his John the Baptist friend.
Posters in place, he tests the mic,
testing, testing, testing.

It was an old one that worked,
for old competitors
in times of traps and sidecars,
ponies and asses tied to rings,
on the walls that American dollars built
to bound the churches
that famine emigration built,
after families gave way to fields
and property made its way into prayers.

All more difficult now,
getting them to stand.
His words fall among the noise of car doors.
He is undeterred.
'They're afraid to show their faces,'
he continues,
lashing at absent opponents.

His voice fades
in the wake of people-carriers,
four-wheel drives
and the Angelus,
a hearse arrives.
Respect the dead.
He arranges to grieve.

Michael D. Higgins

'Never upset a funeral.'
A neighbour gone to meet his maker,
or so they say.
'Sad business all this,
soon it will only be leaflets.'

The man who never had a visitor

They all knew about him
but nobody ever spoke
to the man who never had a visitor
in St Teresa's Ward.
He had come so long ago,
nobody could remember.

It was the neighbours who brought him in.
They heard,
on a strange night,
of a high tide.

He spoke occasionally to the bushes,
or arranging the flowers in vases,
he would be heard to whisper:
But I know, I know,
why I did it.

In the village the story was well known
of the man who'd burned his wife's house.
Together they'd lived for thirty years
without benefit of chick or child,
but he would look at her
in a slow way that they both knew
was love in a time when softness was not allowed,
and the day he found her
stretched in front of the fire,
the tongs grasped in her hand,
he screamed and ran from the house.

It was poitín that made the funeral pass.
The neighbours shovelled out the clay

from his mother's grave,
and one dead lover met another,
and it was poitín too that did it,
they said.

Weeping in the corner of the bar,
he could take it no more,
and never returned home.

The priest, a young man, came
and brought him home.
Pull yourself together, Colie, he said.
Life must go on.

But all he could see was the dresser,
and the two plates where she'd left them,
and the two mugs,
and the two chairs.

*There was two of everything,
there will be one of nothing.*
He screamed,
and ran outside,
the man whose lover had died.

He cast the petrol at the gable thatch.
And as his house burned, he fell to his knees,
and tears came,
and he shook and screamed.
They said it was the poitín,
but all he said was
*I will not let it be.
There was two of everything,
There will be one of nothing.*

And the neighbours saw the flames
of the house of the man
whose lover was gone.
My God, they said, *he must be mad,*
to burn his cosy little house.
And they brought him here,
on a strange night,
of a high tide. And
they all knew about him,
but nobody ever spoke
to the man who never had a visitor
in St Teresa's Ward.
He had come so long ago,
nobody could remember.

And in the village they didn't speak
of the terrible things
that happened on a strange night
of a high tide,
when a man went mad
and burned his house,
screaming only
There was two of everything,
There will be one of nothing.
There are many things better
left unsaid,
and some poor people best
forgotten.

Toes

for my son Michael Edward

Watching the sole of your foot
curled,
I see in the perfection
of its shape
a possibility
of belief
that no random collision
of fact
gave me the feelings
I encounter
as I gaze on those small toes
in perfect shape
as you sleep.

No piece of chance
or probability
can explain
my feeling,
which overflows,
my son,
my love,
my frail hope
of belief
recovered.

Questions without answers

Thinking
in private,
overcome
by the loneliness of pain,
in the distance
a man hauling a bucket
of concrete
on a nearby site
seems
suddenly
very significant.

What is it
that I am leaving?
The sudden beauty
of the known,
dull and predictable,
assaults all the senses.
Every blade of grass
a miracle,
newly invested
with a tapestried
wonder.

Thinking,
on that bad night in hospital,
that I might die,
it was a question
I feared.
After the decay of flesh,
could there be

a holding on
of hope against that fear
that, after all the pain,
the time spent
will be alone,
infinite
loneliness.

The rock-wedged flower
of the Burren
exists alone.
The pain reduces life
to being
a piece of meat,
a mechanical system,
dislodged of hope,
abused.

Not in charge of any choice
of faith,
in stillness,
the lost opportunities for softness
haunt
and give way to a glimmer
of light
in a small corner
of the despairing dark.
The miracle
is in this moment
of the fundamental question.

Are we the children
of some great cosmic
conflict?

Are we the children
of some great unfinished
dream?
Are we the flimsy pieces
of some great unfinished
symmetry?
There would be no answers.

The child's grief will pass.
The spouse's loss will last
for a longer season,
resonant
of a thousand shared
moments.

There is no evasion
of the concentration
on the question required
for answer
in this moment
alone.

Again it comes,
the suggestion
that the answer is in a question,
but the frightened mind
flies back and forth
in terror.
What if the question had no answer,
or had an answer
for which I am too late?

Now, it is necessary,
in desperation,

to throw all cerebral pretence
aside
and, in humility,
ask
if one could be sure
of some old connection
following
between the unavoidable
rot
of the body
and the resilient
spirit.

Black and barren,
a bucket of concrete
lifted by a man
begins the story
of a new day
on a site next door,
a story whose tedious finish
will succeed me.
I need a miracle now
to save
my own belief
in a renewable
season of fire.

Turning from the window,
I weep for the futility
of questions without answers.
I must have this space
but, in all the smaller
gestures,
I will look,
in whatever time is allowed,

for magic moments
where little statements
between questions and answers
   are made,
bright coals
worth the raking,
embers of the season of fire
where my miracle will come.

My terror shared,
my fear
bespeaks
a life of senses
beyond
a speck of dust
and, more than that,
the spark that flickers
will become a flame
shared
in collective concerns,
humanity defined,
set alight
from a fire source
older than the sun.
The answer
is in the flame collective.
No longer am I alone,
and dawn breaks.

On the long night
of my lonely pain,
my miracle,
born in a moment of terror,
blazes
with the gift of seeing

the beauty
of the ordinary.
I am making my way
home.
I hear the words
Take care.

Our Lady of the Trolleys

I am leaving my flowers
to Our Lady of the Trolleys.
They will not last;
nothing outlasts her.
Effervescent,
ceaselessly young,
she deserves my potted plants.

The storyteller

for Tom Murphy

That first man who stood
on a stone
did not grope his way
through the forest
of coy images.
He allowed no requirements
of resonance
to delay his shout
of wonder.

It was passion
that pushed him
past the cowed group
of the curious,
beaten into expectation
of necessary ritual.

And, when he gripped them
with his silences,
they felt a tremor
and the stir of blood,
a jet of urine,
all made bearable
with a long sigh.

The coming out,
the going in,
of the story
followed no rules
written by clerks.

There were no preparatory flourishes
for what was wonderful.

From that moment
they knew
the origin of magic,
and the word,
from a man
who took the risk,
defied the rules and,
standing on a stone,
made a story.
They said, unlike the seers,
he was like God
but made them all divine.

Discourse of crows on a late-winter morning

Their cruciformed arrival
is succeeded
by the making
in cacophony
of their thin black line
of defiance
on a high-tension wire.

Singly they make swirls
of negation.
The cruciform preface
to their linear gesture
is recovered for but a moment,
then noisily lost
in unremitting chaos.

The sound of their rejection
is conclusive.
Silence now defines the morning.

III

The Gaze Not Averted

During the 1970s and 1980s, I decided that staying within the boundaries of academia was limiting. At an educational level, I was, with others, stretching back to rural Ireland in the west, through extra-mural classes from the university, in an area that had Letterkenny as its northern border, Shannon as its southern edge and was bounded by Athlone in the east.

Immense changes involving civil liberties were being argued for at home, and in Central America peasant liberation struggles were underway. A regional church of the poor was gaining strength and challenging political conservatism and dictatorship supported by the military. In Africa, Julius Nyerere had not yet been defeated by the International Monetary Fund and the World Bank. In South Africa, apartheid was being confronted, and that confrontation had international support, led by the brave people who made up the anti-apartheid movement, and of course, the women who sustained a picket for what seemed an eternity: the Dunnes Stores workers.

When I look back at my notes from this period, I am mindful of what served as a warning: Hans Magnus Enzensberger's reference in his essay 'Reflections before a Glass Cage' to 'Tourists of the Revolution'. I quoted this essay in my speech in Helsinki in acceptance of the Seán MacBride Peace Prize of the International Peace Bureau. The essay raised the importance of authenticity, and the trap of what might descend into a voyeurism of conflict and oppression, even torture. I wrote then that the gaze not only must not be averted but the life of the observer must be allowed to change, if one has witnessed the bodies of the assassinated, the mutilations, the inscriptions of death and torture. In that moment of the gaze, an obligatory discourse is called into being.

Always too there was the leaving. Having chosen to take the suffering of one's contemporaries on this fragile and threatened planet into oneself – be it in El Salvador, Chile, Turkey or Somalia – one was changed forever.

Beyond the I

Beyond the I,
there is a golden space,
a shared place,
not in any sky,
no fantasy
escape.

And getting there
requires
a frightening journey
through the gaze
of the other.

To see your seed
in every child's eye
and feel that every wrinkle
in a worn hand
was your own skin
gone dry
requires a journey
that few may take.

For, once begun,
the terrifying gaze
requires
the journey be complete.
That look
in all the children's eyes
will start a fire
in the heart
that no private words
or gesture

of limb or lip
can quench.

In the first stumbling
you may be helped
by allies
for a part
of that journey
through the first challenge.

But, alone,
you must make it through
the fire
where the death of the I
is required,
to the blinding light,
where, unsteady and weak,
you appear
bent,
near-broken.

But all hands combine
in the space of light
and beckon,
all human,
not one I,
but occupants of a shared space where,
at last,
all hearts can beat
together,
that space
of no difference
beyond the I
where life no longer defies
death.

And a great unity
brings peace
with all creation,
defiled
no longer
by the I.

Take care

In the journey to the light,
the dark moments
should not threaten.
Belief
requires
that you hold steady.
Bend, if you will,
with the wind.
The tree is your teacher,
roots at once
more firm
from experience
in the soil
made fragile.

Your gentle dew will come
and a stirring
of power
to go on
towards the space
of sharing.

In the misery of the I,
in rage,
it is easy to cry out
against all others
but to weaken
is to die
in the misery of knowing
the journey abandoned
towards the sharing

of all human hope
and cries
is the loss
of all we know
of the divine
reclaimed
for our shared
humanity.
Hold firm.
Take care.
Come home
together.

Foxtrot in San Salvador

In the Camino Royale,
at the edge of the pool,
they are dancing the foxtrot
in full dress,
keeping the show on the road.

The violins
are not weeping
in sympathy
with the blood red leaves
of the bougainvillea tree.

The chlorinated water
shimmers,
carrying,
occasionally,
the shadows of the gloved waiters,
whose brown fingers never
touch the cocktails.
Their white gloves
caress the crystal waist
of each glass until
the explosion
rocks the pylon.

The darkness babble
is of irritation
until the candelabra light
to a resounding
cheer
that is backed

by the cheerful monotone
of the standby
generator.

At the edge of the *favela*,
young boys are running
for cover
in a river
of mutually terrified
brown faces.

The shots ring out
and my heart follows them.
Shadows,
the jeeps roar
in the distance.

From the pool
comes the sound
of a polonaise.

Black Tuesday

for Norma Elena

On that black Tuesday,
I saw you
move from the edge of the crowd
where Daniel was speaking
to the *militantes*.
For some, his words were lost.
Enrico had left the night before.
Sitting, head in hand,
his guitar between his legs,
he gave me his only other
possession,
a Juventad Sandinista copy,
shared with Rosario,
his girl;
and he wrote,
For my Irish friends
in bad times
but asking them to remember
just causes
must, in the end, succeed.

And, when we exchanged an *abrazo*
your eyes filled with tears
and the dark mahogany of your hair
fell around your face
and the frame that the gods built
around the lungs
that sang in July, nineteen seventy-nine,
as the last Somoza flew out,
shook and trembled.

But then,
on that black Tuesday,
you were strong.
Walking away, your head was high,
decorated with its band
of red and black;
for you knew there is no going back
and you will sing again,
Nicaragua, Nicaraguita,
when those with blood on their hands,
sheltering behind the lace gloves
of La Donna Violetta Barros de Chamorro,
have gone.
You were no voice for hire.
The *campesinos* know your soul.
Abroad, it will be singing.
Norma Elena,
you will come home.

Goodbye Mr Michael

On a night in Amasya
necklaced with the tombs
of the memorable,
pockmarked with stones,
the mayor was lamenting,
to me his subversive visitor,
that the old days were gone.

Time was
they would kill a pig each year;
they had meat
once a year,
the mayor was lamenting.

And earlier that day,
at lunch, the prosecutor was citing
crimes against the Turkish Constitution.
From Red Fatsa
he was demanding
two hundred and fifty-nine death sentences.

Carrying a bag at night,
fighting for the shoe polishing in the morning
with competitive brothers,
little Fikri said
Goodbye Mr Michael.

On television
General Evren spoke for the length of two episodes of
    Dallas;
in the hotel I was packing again,
for my return home.

Pol Pot in Anlon Veng

In the *Bangkok Post*
Pol Pot is breaking his silence.
From Anlon Veng
he does not reminisce
of millions of piled skulls,
no nightmare image
from the killing fields
obtrudes.

He is finished,
he says,
with politics.

He is a nationalist still
who has conviction
and time left
to hate Vietnam.
When regret might be expected
he announces
he is ill.
He tells the *Bangkok Post* he is dying.

Waiting for death,
unlike the millions
who fed a monster's dream.
In polite space
he is interviewed.

On its front page
the *Bangkok Post* tells us
that the baht is in freefall,

that an American president
has called from *Air Force One*
to assure us
that he loves Thailand.

Under the mango tree

When they gather under the mango tree
it is of survival they dream.
There is no long past,
no victories jog the senses,
nor can memory recall
a moment of defeat.

When bells ring

No bells rang in Bethlehem,
no voices sang of angels,
when a child was born through pain
to Palestinians made afraid.

Breath of ox and ass gave warmth,
shared a shelter in refusal times,
a sharing that made divine
a space of life and no difference.

When bells now ring around the world,
they sound for ox and ass,
and exiles dispossessed,
for all those made afraid.

Nor is it yet for peace that voices sing,
behind closed doors the words divide,
and whispered fear makes hate behind a wall,
where nothing can be shared.
They wait for peace.

But breath of ox and ass gave warmth two thousand years
    ago,
shared a shelter in refusal times.
That sharing made divine
a space of life and no difference.

And the trees wept

Together they made a shelter,
among the children of Abraham,
at the time of the promise of His coming.

In the Temple He asked if it were to be a battle
of olive cypress and cedar.
For He knew even then
that the branches of palm would be strewn
for His arrival in glory.
And that at another time the olive trees would be torn
from the ground to make way for a wall
between the children of Abraham.

And that the cedar would be burned from the sky,
in a great rage between neighbours.
And the olive, the cypress, and the cedar wept
among the children of Abraham,
and made tears that fell
on the arid soil of Palestine,
where the trees longed to make a shelter,
together among the children of Abraham.

And elsewhere bells were ringing,
and mirth overflowed with abandon
in a great forgetting
of His words on the Mount,
of the need to make peace
among the children of Abraham.

And Jesus joined with all the Prophets
and added his tears to the tears of the trees,

in the arid times,
in Palestine, among the children of Abraham.

Minister for Justice addresses new Irish citizens who were previously non-persons seeking asylum or work

The language will be your test.
Even from you today I have overheard it,
the wrong stuff:
words like kindness,
softness,
goodness.
Those soft words,
cut them out.

When I present you to His Excellency,
remember your lessons.
You are grateful to be allowed
to be citizens among the confident Irish,
the rich, confident European Irish.

You will work without ceasing,
your children will never cost a penny to the state,
you will avoid agitators,
even if the Prophet did not,
you will turn the other cheek
to racist insults.

And when he smiles on you,
she will know
how grateful you are,
how grateful you will always remain.

Michael D. Higgins

That is how it has to be;
I have made it so.
And in the end,
you are welcome
to a cup of tea,
new, useful Irish citizens.

Cead míle fáilte.

IV

Of Irony and Insufficiency

Erving Goffman's *The Presentation of Self in Everyday Life* was the text of a course that, as a young lecturer in the United States, I taught at the end of the 1960s. The professor also required students to break and report on a social norm, not a moral norm. The result was chaos, but also a revelation of the taken-for-granted nature of events in spaces previously unquestioned. It was to be much later, when I myself was living a life in the public space, that I recalled this valuable dramaturgical perspective as it applied to Ireland and Irish rituals.

For a republic, Ireland has a very large number of chains of office. Indeed, I recall events I attended as mayor of Galway, where great pleasure was expressed at 'the presence of the chain here tonight'. Ireland is a country where a sense of humour is not only necessary but also respected and appreciated.

The verses from the midlands of such regional poets as Patrick Higgins, a contemporary of Percy French, are wonderful examples of the use of the new language, English, as an instrument for exposing the pretentiousness of new fashions and commodities.

Irony is only one of the great gifts of the poet Paul Durcan. Some of Paul's poems discomfited a society, sections of which had been anaesthetised by smugness and individualism. But while they may have raised blisters on the complacent, they were delivered with a compassion that drove his poetic instinct.

Such poems as 'Making love outside Áras an Uachtaráin' confirmed that a major poet had arrived. Some of his other poems, such as 'Wife who smashed television gets jail' showed his power of irony in deconstructing a society that regarded indissoluble unions as chosen by God for the Irish and within which, if there were difficulties, you could always put on the kettle. After all, that is what they did in *The Riordans*. Of course, by the time *Fair City* had brought us into the new century, Carrigstown had taken to the drink.

Irony on its own, however, can bring us only so far. Dealing with the absurdities and contradictions of life requires a humour that must also be accessible.

A race-week reflection in the university city of Galway, 1970

Evening breaks over the fast-greening
copper dome of Galway's cathedral.
In Peter Michael's, mirth is forsaken for grief,
however brief,
as funeral time approaches.
Bury the dead properly.
The widow arranges to weep.
In another room a drunken father
welcomes an accidental son,
born into a world he'll never understand.
Students pass, carrying books and jotters,
notes half-carelessly taken from
the yellowed files
of professors who have long lost interest.
The funeral emerges.
Draw the blinds.
Respect the dead.
Popular man that.
Fair amount of cars.
From Castlebar, they say.

Downtown, the lawyers,
with long legal faces,
fresh from the High Court in circuit,
are trying to decide whether to leave the tavern
to travel for oysters in Clarinbridge
or to settle for the Claddagh Grill.
Exchanging stories loudly, they command respect,
as they should – people of substance.
Wearers of wigs by morning,

147

their Adam's apples scarcely give as the afternoon claret
salves their memories of clients.

We must remember it is Race Week,
when all Galway comes alive,
and dead expectations of sex,
or even love, resurface.
Thin-lipped Julia, sipping brandy in a corner,
from a glass that intimidates,
casts eyes half-furtively
at a loud-mouthed farmer, strayed in,
whom, more likely, she should despise.
Thinking carefully, she turns her body,
no longer beautiful but protected,
in the direction of those more likely respectable,
and sighs.

In the Cellar Bar
you who called yourself 'Mate'
are bumming the price of pints
from sleveens half your worth,
balancing yourself to ask,
in your own well-turned phrase,
How're you fixed for the rough touch?
Yours the lesser request,
paid for with a wit that was not acquired
at Chamber of Commerce meetings,
but in the flux of life itself.
You will be missed by those who loved or cared,
not by the hucksters,
for whom the till rings loud.

Estate agents, insurance brokers and bankers,
this is your week.
Above all others, you talk indiscreetly

of looking after your figures
and playing squash –
adequate replacements for intellect.
But let us not be bitter.
Are your wives not beautiful,
at a price?
They concentrate
on not letting you down in public
as they spray sherry
from glasses held in inexperienced hands,
forgetting that one occasion
when ribs were broken in their rush
towards a visiting Irish-American president
at a garden party at Áras an Uachtaráin.

In Riley's pub
a few older men with red faces,
indicating the evening of a life
devoted to porter and patriotism,
look uncomfortably at their successors
in green second-hand jackets,
who talk of republicanism by day,
and at night, being consistent,
whet their thirst
and, not forgetting principle,
sing 'Joe Hill'
for benefit of passion and profit.

In the Great Southern Hotel
a man regarded as mad
for interrupting a bishop in his cathedral,
saying he'd heard it all before,
seized by Knights of Columbanus in Christ's House,
and cured by ECT in Ballinasloe,
tells American tourists he wants them

to join with him
in saying the Rosary in the foyer
for the boys in Vietnam.
Chaos reigns among the bags
as porters struggle
to defeat the prayers.
He is told that he is barred,
the hotel made safe for winners at the races,
where once the sleveens shouted
when Máirtín Mór McDonagh's horse came home
in the Galway Plate in 1934.
Lead him in yourself, Mr Máirtín,
they to whom Máirtín Mór gave a free coffin
for a lifetime in his service,
owning them in life,
boxing them in death.
Tonight his spirit will no doubt rejoice
with those who've come for the Galway Races.

Walking past your great stone cathedral,
I cannot but think of you, cross Michael of Galway,
pompous heir of the Apostles.
You saved us your presence this night,
alone at home on the night of the Galway Races.
More charitable perhaps
than they say,
you stayed at home,
musing over the irrelevancies
you would inflict on Sunday;
lonely, friend of none save those
too tired or too cowed to question
a metaphysics long outdated,
you pour a glass of wine or port
and remember better days,
when Russell was proved in error

to the applause of reverend fathers, sisters,
ladies and gentlemen,
two hundred nuns
and a hundred apprentice Franciscans,
on St Thomas Aquinas' Day
in the Aula Maxima of UCG.
Brilliant but wrong, Cathal Daly said,
to tumultuous applause.
But you outdid Cathal in your day
in natural law,
arguing for the distinction between false teeth and condoms.

And now I must return
to the irrelevancy of my own earned madness,
look fearfully at students, uninterested,
wanting their introduction to commerce,
blessed with unconcern,
anxious to serve, escape –
who knows, grow rich.

I have exhausted my concession
and it is time to go and take my place
where the mad and foolish lodge.
And, after all, the morning will break on a new day
after the Galway Races.

Bank manager faints at the mayor's ball

The mayor was dancing with her golden chain,
not dangling,
but nestling on her ample bosom,
when she turned to the bank manager and said,
Come on outa that and give us a dance.

He was a frightened man
but he knew his duty.
We'll make it a slow one, she said,
and he trembled.

Three brandies later,
for the benefit of the bank and a safe branch,
his call came.

Hold me tight, she said.
*I love a tight squeeze for the waltz,
and I've no time
for this highfalutin stuff.*

The first citizen and the bank
danced cheek to cheek.
every usurious fibre was tested
as she breathed on his bald head.
She joked occasionally as he laughed
and missed a step.

*Oh, if I had you in my time
on the kitchen floor*, she said,
I'd give you a one-two-three

you'd never forget.

The perspiration beaded his brow;
his legs turned to jelly.
His eyes blurred as he sank to the floor.
Dear Jesus, he's fainted, the first lady said.
What lack of respect for the dignity of my office.
But, then, I've never trusted the banks.

They picked him up and said he needed air,
but, taking her handbag and walking away,
she coldly looked at them all,
and simply said,
with all the dignity of the office,

It's a poor thing at the mayor's ball
when the Chain can't waltz with safety
with those who for our own account
bought the little box we carry it in.
It isn't air he needs
but a box.

Blowing her nose, she laughed,
and the band played on
at the mayor's ball.

Jesus appears in Dublin in 1990 at the Port & Docks Board site

It created a sensation.
The TV cameras were there.
Everybody was weeping
when Jesus appeared in Dublin at the Port & Docks Board
    site in 1990.
The ageing prime minister tried to be photographed with
    him,
but Jesus was having none of it.

I've come myself, he said,
for I'm tired of sending my mother,
and I wanted to say how pleased I am
that you've stopped all that nonsense
they press-released from me on the Mount.
The embargo was scarcely over
when I knew it was all a dreadful mistake.
The truth is I'm European now like you.

Tough measures are necessary in these difficult times,
as you busy men know.
Let the children be without books.
Words and books are dangerous things.
Let the aged die in silence.
They talk too much.

And get rid of all that stuff of ripening youth.
Or the roots of the tree will give way
under the rot of their fallen expectations.

The sick are not really sick;
we all know that in our hearts.
You work, you live, you tell them,
and you're right.
Those old solidarities are evil,
it is the I that counts.

And all that business about the money-lenders
in the Temple:
the truth is I never meant it.
They were of your kind,
far too smart,
far too quick
for me.

I confess.
I confess.
Try to forgive me.
And even my mother knows I've wronged you.
And she will come again to you all,
and I'll try to be a European.

The tears flowed down his white Caucasian face.
The crowd threw themselves on the ground,
littered with Coca-Cola cans,
and looked up at the sky and said,
Oh God,
thank you for sending your son
and preparing us for 1992.

The minister's black car

Still, children.
Stand in line.
Quiet, children.
Be ready when it comes,
the minister's black car.

Sister Gabrielle is excited.
She hasn't slept a wink.
God forgive her,
she couldn't concentrate at Mass,
thinking of it all:
the new extension,
the opening, and
the minister's black car

Pulling herself together,
she tells them again,
Be ready,
Clap when it comes.
Clap when you see it, just
clap, children, clap for
the minister's black car.

Suddenly she sees it.
Clap, children, clap.
It's here.
Clap for the minister's black car.

The minister's leaving her car.
Clap, children,
for the minister leaving her car.

The minister's smiling at you, children.
Clap, children, clap
for the minister's lovely teeth.

The minister's going inside.
Clap, children, clap.
The minister's eating a biscuit.
Clap, children, clap.
Sister Gabrielle is overcome:
her big day.
The minister's coming towards her.
You're Sister Gabrielle.
I've heard so much about you.
The children clap for Sister Gabrielle.

Gabrielle's passing out.
Where are the toilets, Sister?
   she hears in a daze.
The minister's going to the toilet,
   she screams.
Clap, children, clap.
The minister's spending a penny.

The minister's car is purring.
The children are lined outside.
Quiet, children.
Stand in line.
Cheer, children.
Remember, not only when you see her,
not only after she closes her door,
not only after she smiles at me,
until you see the dust.
Cheer, children.
Clap, children, clap
for the minister's black car.

An Irish architect
reflects on his success

Smooth-shaven and with a hint of purple,
mouth firm and wry-lipped with success,
hair silvered, lovingly jowled,
dentures secure, fingertips touching,
and fat,
a partner.

Half-spectacles perched on a shining nose
for being seen,
he corrects his own amplification,
beautiful tones, perfectly adjusted,
right amount of bass,
he talks of contracts
that are a challenge.

Credit card dangling,
his instrument
of purchase,
flaunted
in company that cannot refuse,
even if it intimidates
with its youth.

In days before he went pink,
he wore a beard,
was seen
in Wellingtons and mud,
on special days, a hard hat
and armfuls of drawings,
for he,

they said,
had a lovely touch.

He did not choose to go pink.
It crept over him   ·
like success
and, in that mad transition,
he traded in
his beard
for a bow-tie
that was meant to suggest
maturity
with just a hint
of eccentricity.

He did not get where he is today
from foundations of boardroom lunches,
by making a virtue
of dirt or clients,
and his raucous laugh gives way
to a most attractive wheeze
as memories fill his eyes with water,
or is it gin? Who cares?
Flesh of face making no vulgar movement
but now gently rocking itself
across the lovely dimples of middle years.

When he was young, he was known
for his good eye
and clean lines.
In kitchens, he'd shared moments with couples
who even talked of extensions,
first dissipations of love
and madness of youth.

Staring into the distance, he recalls
the moment of success.
'Pink & Partners' he'd put on his plate,
and everyone wanted him.
Why have anybody else, they said,
when you can have Pink?

At Christmas, in bistros, they even sang
a song for him
that he grew to love.
I once was green but now I'm pink,
and they humoured him
when the truth no longer could be denied
that he'd gone purple.

It came in flashes
that frightened him
as friends
surreptitiously
talked of heart
but, in the end,
it was a satisfaction
to know
that, when he took his slide-rule home
for the last time
from Pink & Partners,
he'd changed the colour
of his profession
and his universe
for an even greater success,
transition,
special appointment
to God
for renovation
of low-cost housing

for poorer classes
in heaven.
It was a new beginning
in time, he thought.
He'd get to tackle
the Mansions.
He gave a long sigh –
why not? –
at his success.

Revivalists

At the meeting some decided
that for the Revival
they would not have sex
except for procreation,
with eyes averted.
Others were in favour
of lots of it,
to build an army
for the Revival.

At 'any other business'
after the nasty exchanges
about the true structure of grammar,
a civil servant with glasses demanded the floor.
I know I'm stepping out of line –
he blushed as he said it –
but I want to talk of knickers
and long johns.

Some were shocked;
they spilled their balls of malt.
'They should be made of tweed,' he said,
'until the Revival is complete.
To remind us through the scratching
that we are suffering
for the Revival.'

The numbed silence gave way
and the sound of cheers broke
up from the basement
out on to Molesworth Street,
where a crowd had gathered.

'They've gone for the tweed knickers' –
the whispers ran like wildfire –
'for the Revival.'

The Guards, who'd all changed their names,
thousands of civil servants,
members of semi-state bodies,
professors and eccentric clerics
who were gathered in Kildare Street
danced a set together
in celebration.

Dancing outside their very own Dáil,
they felt rightly proud.
They were making history.
The new nation had taken a decision
for the Revival,
and they shouldered high
the man with glasses
who dreamed the dream
and made the motion
under 'any other business'
that made it possible for them all
to wear tweed knickers
and scratch
for the Revival.

Ritualists

They are bending towards the rising sun
Immersed
In body-burning rituals
At the evening of life
Migrants from a life made tedious
Far from the season
They have hoarded their dream
Of sea and sand and waves and sun

They are bending towards the sinking sun
In prayer
In the occupied desert
Above the oil that is calling the stranger
Praying
For the defeat of the stranger infidel
Bending in desperation
For loss of a life that is ending
Bending in prayer for defeat of the enemy

To the bending the sun is perhaps indifferent
The sun is waiting
Knowing
That it will witness
The defeat
Of the body burning and the prayers

And as to conclusions
The sun must know
That it too
Will expire
Not lost in any sense

Simply over
Like life
Like body burning
And prayers

Its place in space remains
Endures
Utopia

V

Of Friendship, Loss and Hope

It was Aristotle who said that friendship makes an ethical demand greater than that of justice. This is a truth that should not be avoided. For example, John O'Donohue's friendship was for me a rare and precious gift. His energetic company, his scintillating mind, and above all his humble and inspiring sanctification of nature and the ordinary meant that any room was filled by his presence, any conversation made memorable.

Visiting me in hospital in 2005, he spoke of his draft lecture for Professor John Dillon's Plato seminar in Trinity College. His lecture was on 'Possibility', which is why I have given my poem that title, in his honour. John's premature passing was a great loss, as were the passings of Dr Noel Browne, Dr David Thornley and Dr Paddy Leahy – all of whom I knew well. In all these passings, and others, however, the ideas of those passing on did not die, nor will they.

I was to experience an extraordinary passage in friendship through the time I spent with Dr Paddy Leahy abroad some months before his death. Over an extraordinary period of about ten days, this brave humanist looked back over his life as a young medical student in Dublin, as a Tipperary minor hurler, and as the young but courageous secretary of a golf club in England from which he resigned because of its anti-Semitism. He relived his time running a free medical clinic in Ballyfermot, where he sought to make modern medicine and advice available to all – his efforts not only not assisted by the bureaucracy but opposed by them.

We spoke in that faraway place where he stayed of Shelley, Byron, Keats and Dylan Thomas, of *The Razor's Edge* and Ingersoll. I have such a strong recollection of the connection Paddy made between the life and the poetry. When he got tired, he quoted Monk Gibbon's 'The Last Thing', with its powerful end lines: 'Go bravely, for where so much greatness and gentleness have been already, you should be glad to follow.'

In all such conversations with friends, something changed for me. In John O'Donohue's case, his enthusiastic assertion of the divinity involved in nature's renewal was a powerful message not only for me but for so many others, signalling the importance of the symmetry of a life lived in nature, as opposed to the violent degradation of nature. The way in which he combined possibility, prophecy, cultural and human rights and the utopian tradition marked an important step away from the destructive individualism that was becoming the norm, and the beginning of a journey of hope, and intergenerational love and solidarity, which we all must share.

The truth of poetry

for Mark Patrick Hederman

In its beginning
the truth of poetry is a light,
sheltered,
yet no mere spark of a moment,
exhausted,
ephemeral.

The truth of poetry flickers
as the fire takes.
Truth-making feeds the flames,
that blaze again,
becomes beautiful in the light,
and in the fire is seen,
for a moment,
possibility
unquenchable,
transformed,
reborn out of time,
out of decay.
As the flames rise,
the turf expires.

Nor yet is this an answer.
Such fire as truth requires
is from a source inexhaustible.
Such fire as would make of hope
a possibility made inevitable
awaits the lighting.

Michael D. Higgins

Then let us pray,
for those who hope,
that from the raking of the ashes,
and the placing of the seeds,
for a new fire,
and a new day.
In eternal renewal,
such a fire may come,
as lets them see,
even for a while,
the fragile truth of poetry,
revealed,
enough for the going on.

Of possibility

In memory of John O'Donohue

From that wider space
that is imagination,
is made possible
a visual beauty
that dazzles and ensnares.

Deep in that space lies too,
in unreleased expectancy,
versions of a world unborn,
sending shards of light and colour
that make an invitation
to something truly human.

They lodge in memory,
making an inheritance
of possibility not always realised.

And in that site yielded up by memory
to spirit at the end,
it is these shafts
and unrealised suggestions
that endure,
at the end,

making a rich legacy
of possibility.

Of little flowers

Those thousand little flowers
obdure in a wild place,
not using their company
in sheltering moist grasses,
when subjected to an intense examination,
and torn from their meagre soil,
more often have been thrown away,
with their stale water.

It is among the thousand little flowers,
emerging in a quite humility,
love is sprinkled,
without precision,
takes root,
without our taking note.

Survivors of great rages,
against powerful forces,
they draw for life
on what is dislodged,
made moist by accident,
the occasional gaze,
scraps of appreciation,
deepens their colour,
forces a conceit.

And in other times,
not worth the picking,
left in near-obscuring grass,
on occasion
they are exposed in the wrong colour,

made vulnerable
for retrieval.

But more usually they return,
in annual visitation,
indomitable,
embracing the trunk of a tree gone dry,
vindicating a power,
lodged in little things.

The ebbing tide

I have brought my soul to the sea
in turbulent times,
seeking an answer
from the tide.

Skimming a question at its surge,
I ask of its army of souls,
tossed in restless motion,
is it that they prepare for daily battle
with the landlocked living?

And are the pieces left
on the ebbing tide,
the spirit losses of battle,
flotsam and jetsam,
defeated souls?

And must a choice be made
between the marauding souls
that make the restless sea,
and those others under siege,
clinging to the land,
obstinate in defiance,
against the inevitable?

And if a peace were made
between that sea of turbulent souls
and the landlocked discontented,
would the tide not wash with ease
on the compromising sand?

And when the Prophet walked on water,
was he not making that peace
between two armies of lost hope,
one landlocked and unfulfilled,
another restless,
in its marauding infinity,
no end possible?

Just bits and pieces,
strewn after the last tide,
all there is at evening,
remnants of an unending war,
waiting for darkness
and the ebbing tide.

But beneath the stars
and under the gaze of a full moon,
what if I skim a different question?
Will others not in wonder seek
from the still and peaceful water
new gifts from souls
that meet to dance?

No longer in collision,
they listen to an infinite music
made by stars.
And make a prayer
crafted out of time,
infinite.

And my soul laughed and said:
No more time for questions.
Time to return, go home;
time for sleep.
And tomorrow is another day;

we will come again when the tide is in.
And the wind agreed with my soul
as we turned for home
and away
from the ebbing tide.

Memory

As Ricoeur said,
To be removed from memory
is to die twice.
Nor should it be allowed
to make an amnesia
of violence.
An amnesty is enough
for the detail.
And who knows whether,
if in time,
such a healing is possible
as would make an evening
of forgiveness
worth the going on.
We make an affirmation.
The stuff of hope beckons.
Out of the darkness
we step,
and blink into the new light.

Of utopias

Old utopias never die
nor do they fade away.
Born of possibility
out of ancestor traces,
memory gives birth
to imagination.

From a whisper it grows,
and makes a music,
in the quiet places of the heart,
where a new song is made,
soaring above the lesser sounds
of false inevitabilities,
it makes an echo.

Nor is it the vain cry
of a child of reason.
It is a shout at the future,
that is there for the making,
becomes a song
shared by the many
in joyous anticipation.